follow Me

Peter Lays Down His Net

An Easter Story
written by Erik Rottmann

CONCORDIA PUBLISHING HOUSE · SAINT LOUIS

To Aaron Philip

and Aidan Christian:

Sons by birth

and brothers by Baptism.

Based on the gospels of
Matthew, Mark, Luke, and John.

Peter loved Jesus. Everyday he followed wherever Jesus went. If Jesus went inside a house, Peter went inside too. If Jesus traveled to another town, Peter went along. It had been this way ever since Jesus said, **"Follow Me."**

Peter often thought about the first time he met Jesus. He had been fishing with his brother, Andrew, when Jesus walked up and called out to them, "Follow Me." They both dropped their nets and followed. Peter was glad Jesus wanted them to be His apostles.

During their many travels, Peter watched Jesus do miraculous things. He saw Jesus turn a small meal into enough food for thousands of people. He saw Jesus calm a terrible storm by saying simply, "Be quiet!" Peter even saw Jesus heal sick people and make dead people alive again.

Peter knew Jesus was the promised Savior. So when Jesus asked Peter, "Who do you say I am?" Peter quickly answered, **"You are the Christ, the Son of the living God."**

One day Jesus went to **Jerusalem** to celebrate the Passover. Peter and the other disciples went to Jerusalem too.

During the Passover meal, Jesus began to wash His disciples' feet. Peter did not like to see his dear Master doing such a humble job. He thought Jesus ought to have others wash *His* feet instead. So when it was Peter's turn, he asked, "Lord, why are You doing this?"

Jesus answered, "Peter, if I do not wash your feet, we cannot be together any more. Right now, you do not understand why I must do this. But you will understand soon enough."

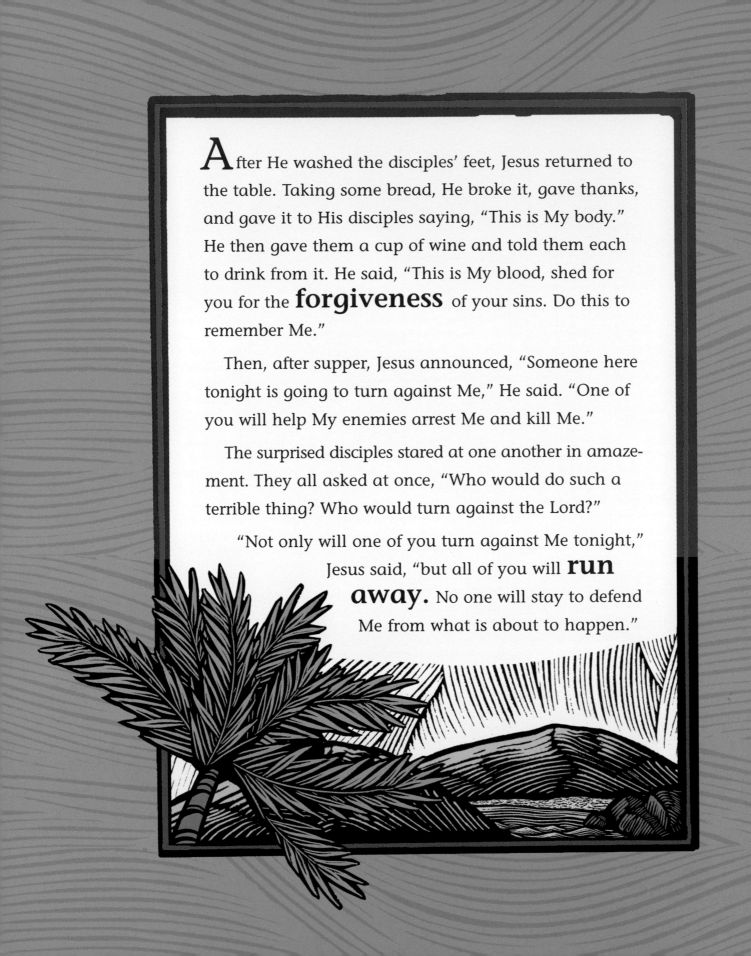

After He washed the disciples' feet, Jesus returned to the table. Taking some bread, He broke it, gave thanks, and gave it to His disciples saying, "This is My body." He then gave them a cup of wine and told them each to drink from it. He said, "This is My blood, shed for you for the **forgiveness** of your sins. Do this to remember Me."

Then, after supper, Jesus announced, "Someone here tonight is going to turn against Me," He said. "One of you will help My enemies arrest Me and kill Me."

The surprised disciples stared at one another in amazement. They all asked at once, "Who would do such a terrible thing? Who would turn against the Lord?"

"Not only will one of you turn against Me tonight," Jesus said, "but all of you will **run away.** No one will stay to defend Me from what is about to happen."

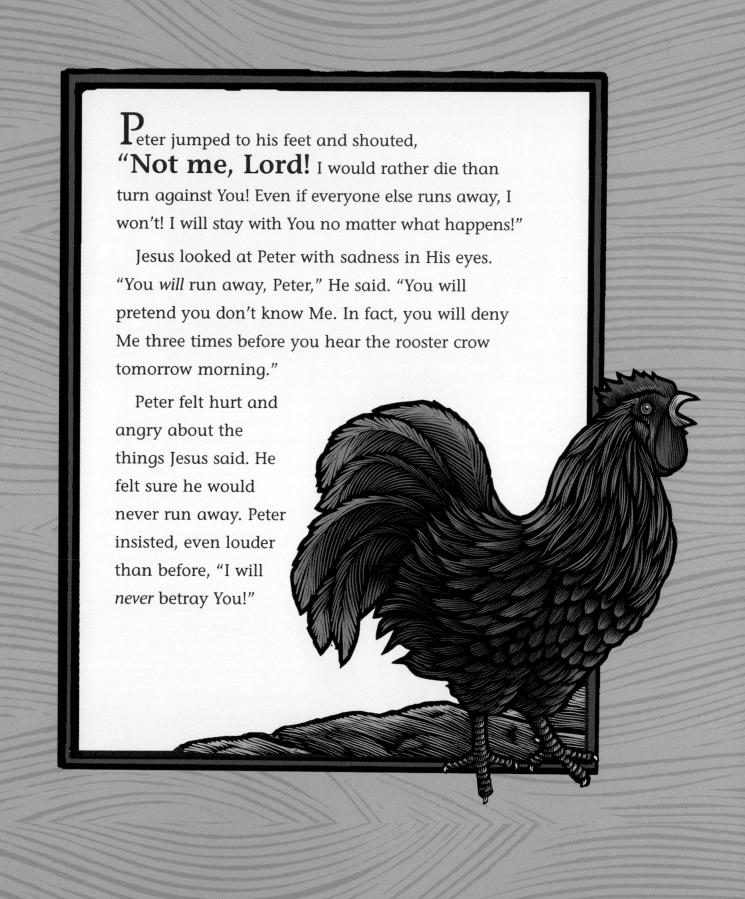

Peter jumped to his feet and shouted, **"Not me, Lord!** I would rather die than turn against You! Even if everyone else runs away, I won't! I will stay with You no matter what happens!"

Jesus looked at Peter with sadness in His eyes. "You *will* run away, Peter," He said. "You will pretend you don't know Me. In fact, you will deny Me three times before you hear the rooster crow tomorrow morning."

Peter felt hurt and angry about the things Jesus said. He felt sure he would never run away. Peter insisted, even louder than before, "I will *never* betray You!"

Then Jesus and some of His disciples walked to a quiet garden and Jesus knelt to pray. While they were there, a disciple named **Judas Iscariot** came into the garden.

Behind Judas was a crowd of people looking for Jesus. These people were Jesus' enemies. And they had come to arrest Him.

Just as Jesus had said—one of His disciples had turned against Him.

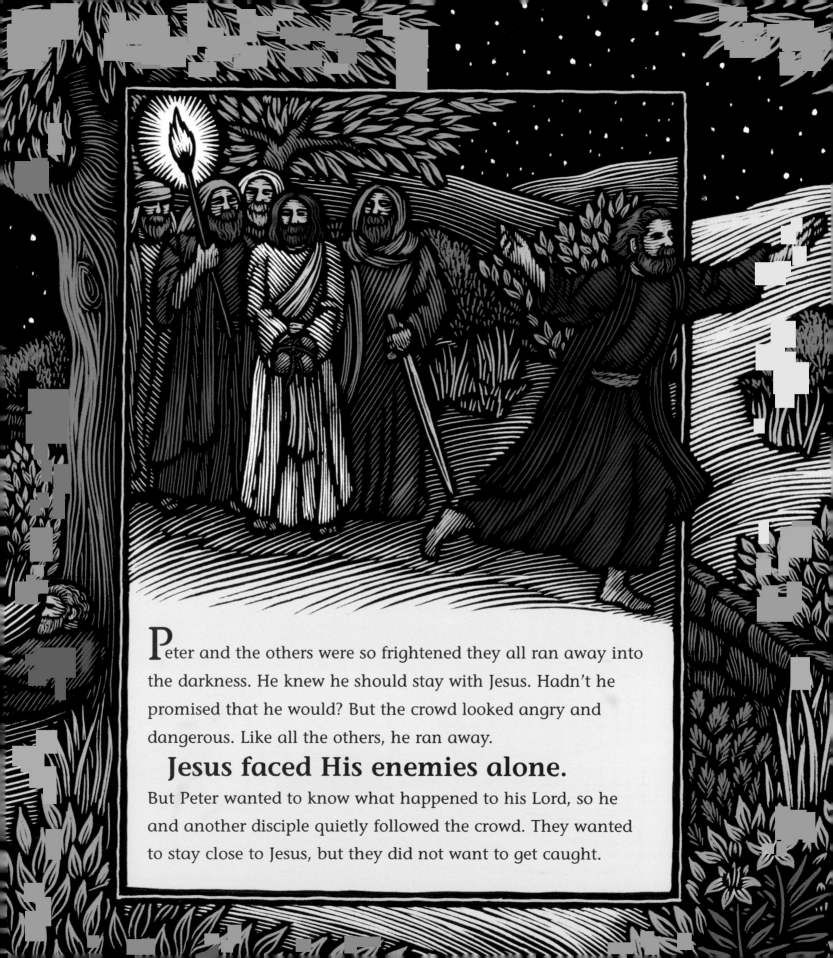

Peter and the others were so frightened they all ran away into the darkness. He knew he should stay with Jesus. Hadn't he promised that he would? But the crowd looked angry and dangerous. Like all the others, he ran away.

Jesus faced His enemies alone.

But Peter wanted to know what happened to his Lord, so he and another disciple quietly followed the crowd. They wanted to stay close to Jesus, but they did not want to get caught.

The crowd took Jesus to the palace of the high priest. The other disciple went in to see what was happening while Peter waited outside.

After a while, a girl opened the door to let Peter in. She asked, "Are you one of the men who follows Jesus?"

The question startled him. He quickly answered, "No, I'm not," and walked away.

Peter felt cold so he stood next to a fire to warm himself. Other people also stood near the fire. One of them looked at Peter and asked, **"Do you follow this Jesus who was arrested?** Are you one of His disciples?"

"Not me," Peter shook his head. "I don't know what you're talking about."

But one of the people had been in the crowd when Jesus was arrested. He asked Peter, "Hey, didn't I see you in the garden with Jesus?"

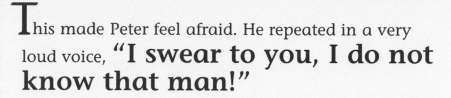This made Peter feel afraid. He repeated in a very loud voice, **"I swear to you, I do not know that man!"**

Just then, Peter remembered what Jesus had said about his denial. He remembered how he had insisted, "Not me, Lord!"

Suddenly a rooster crowed. When Peter heard the sound, he began to cry. Everything had happened exactly as Jesus said it would!

Sad, ashamed, and guilty, Peter ran from the palace courtyard.

Later that day **it was over**. Jesus was nailed to a cross and He died.

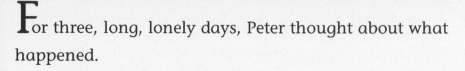

For three, long, lonely days, Peter thought about what happened.

Jesus had been taken away. He was crucified and laid in a tomb. And Peter had done nothing to stop it. In fact, he did the very thing he said he would never do—he had denied Jesus.

Then, on the Sunday after Jesus was crucified, Peter and the other disciples heard wonderful news. Mary and two other women had burst into the room where the men were praying and shouted, "Jesus has risen from the dead! **His tomb is empty! He lives!**"

Peter didn't wait to hear any more. He and another disciple ran to the tomb. The women were right— the tomb was indeed empty.

Jesus is alive!

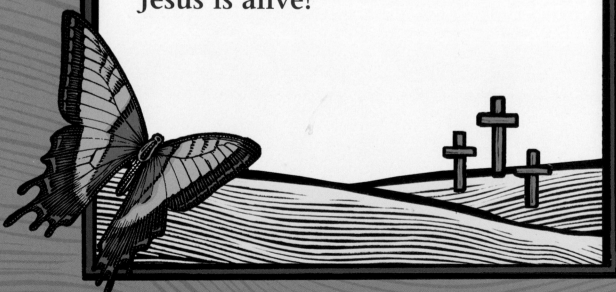

Everyone was talking. The news that Jesus is alive began to spread. Jesus Himself appeared to His disciples to show them He had overcome sin, death, and the devil by His resurrection.

In time, Peter, Andrew, and some of the others went back to work as fishermen.

One morning, as they were heading home after fishing all night, they saw a man waving to them from the shore. The man told them to throw their nets into the water one more time. (They had not caught a single fish that night, but they did what the man said.)

This time, when they pulled their nets from the water, they caught so many fish the nets almost broke. The fishermen looked at the man on the shore in amazement—it was Jesus, their resurrected Lord!

Peter was so excited to see Jesus that he jumped from the boat and swam to Him. The other disciples quickly rowed the boats to the shore to see Him too.

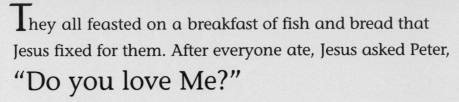

They all feasted on a breakfast of fish and bread that Jesus fixed for them. After everyone ate, Jesus asked Peter, **"Do you love Me?"**

"Do I love You, Lord?" Peter answered. "Yes, I do!"

Jesus said, "Keep following Me, and teach others to follow Me as well." He asked a second time, "Peter, do you love Me?"

Peter wondered, *hadn't Jesus heard him the first time?* Speaking a little more clearly, he answered, "Yes, Lord. You know I love You."

Jesus said, "Take care of the others who follow Me." Then Jesus asked a third time, "Peter, do you love Me?"

Now Peter felt confused. He kneeled in front of Jesus and whispered, "You know me, Lord, just as You know all things. **You know that I love You."**

Jesus grasped Peter's arms and helped him to his feet. Then He said, "Keep following Me, and teach others to follow Me as well."

Peter finally understood. Jesus loved Peter! Jesus loved Peter no matter what! **Jesus died for Peter so his sins would be forgiven.** Jesus rose from the dead so Peter would know He is the way to heaven. Jesus welcomed Peter back into His arms, setting aside and forgetting all the bad things Peter had done.

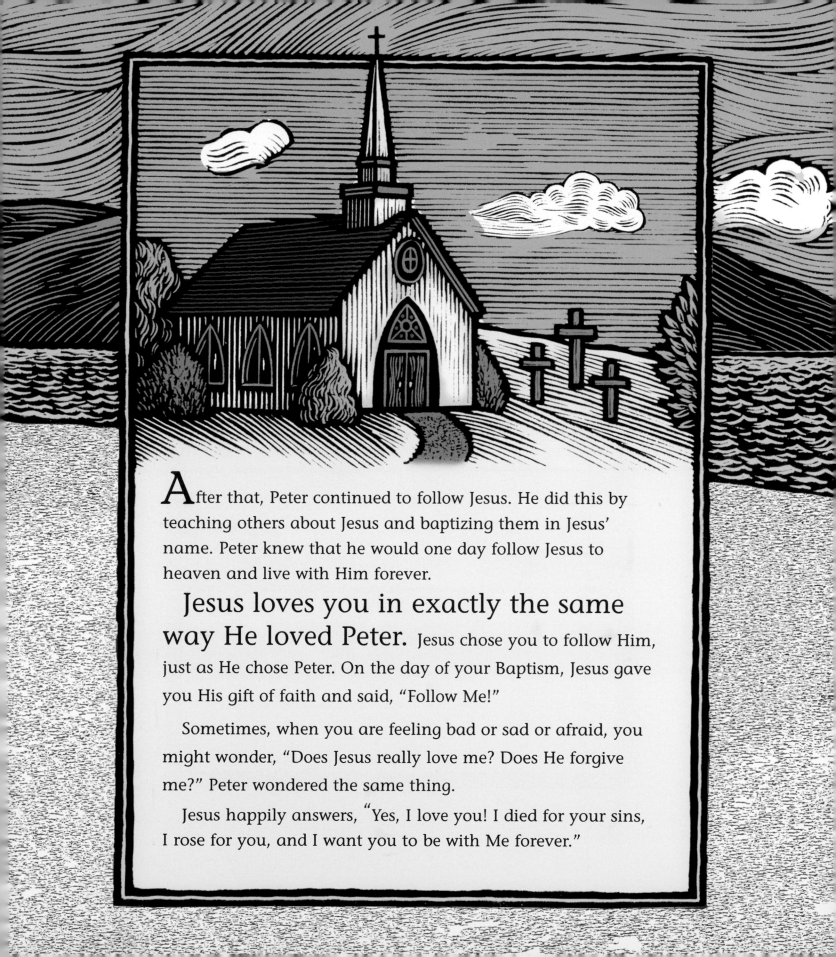

After that, Peter continued to follow Jesus. He did this by teaching others about Jesus and baptizing them in Jesus' name. Peter knew that he would one day follow Jesus to heaven and live with Him forever.

Jesus loves you in exactly the same way He loved Peter. Jesus chose you to follow Him, just as He chose Peter. On the day of your Baptism, Jesus gave you His gift of faith and said, "Follow Me!"

Sometimes, when you are feeling bad or sad or afraid, you might wonder, "Does Jesus really love me? Does He forgive me?" Peter wondered the same thing.

Jesus happily answers, "Yes, I love you! I died for your sins, I rose for you, and I want you to be with Me forever."

Published by Concordia Publishing House
3558 S. Jefferson Avenue, St. Louis, MO 63118-3968
Text copyright © 2004 Erik Rottmann
Illustrations copyright © 2004 Concordia Publishing House

Manufactured in the United States
1 2 3 4 5 6 7 8 9 10 11 12   14 13 12 11 10 09 08 07 06 05 04